60 Selected Poems of

Seo Jeong-Nam

A Gold Beetle's Nostalgia

서정남 시선집(제9집)

풍뎅이의 향수 鄕愁

60 Selected Poems of
Seo Jeong-Nam
A Gold Beetle's Nostalgia

서정남 시선집(제9집)
풍뎅이의 향수 鄕愁

Tr. by Won Eung-Soon

도서출판 조 은
Published by JOEUN Pub.Co.

Preface

I issue the 9th poetic anthology. Why do I write poetry?

The answer is clear-cut. We can't exist without breath, so that's why I have to breathe, to have deeper respiration as a behaviour for being that means to write poetry.

What is called, the original meaning, 'esprit' of Latin language is 'breath' and breath starts from the lungs, with the beating of the heart by breath together, to keep our life, and the lungs correspond to our understanding, the heart corresponds to 'will', so the heavenly secret of my poems in which has been melt through, means that understanding good and practicing it by will is to establish love and peace, happiness, prosperity, and harmony.

For instance, a few lines of my poem, "A Recollection", in such lines as "the heaven filled hungry stomach/ the star's light quenching thirst", these images figuring in the above lines are based on a principle of "correspondence" beyond the ideas of the general parables and symbols. Everyone knows that a piece of poem, the moment making public out of the world, returns to the readers. Therefore sometimes some readers understand my poems and get touched their heart, when I hear them saying so, I can't help deeply moving with their warm concerns. So I stoop to ask a favor of our readers, issuing the poetic anthology to the world even if this poetic anthology does not meet its readers as much to be a wandering language.

Daringly saying by myself, " I write a poem, therefore I exist !"
like Descarte's "Certification for Being" of God.

머리말

아홉 번째로 시집을 펴낸다. 왜 시를 쓰는가? 대답은 명쾌하다. 호흡 없인 살 수없는 존재! 그래서 호흡을 해야 하고 좀 더 깊은 호흡을 하기 위한 생존행위가 곧 詩 쓰기에 매달리는 이유이다.

이른바, 시 정신 'esprit'의 라틴어의 원뜻이 '호흡'이라는 사실과 호흡은 허파(lung)로 하며, 호흡에 의하여 심장(heart)의 박동이 함께 이루어짐으로써 생명이 유지되는데, 허파는 이해(understanding)에 상응하고 심장은 의지(will)에 상응하며, 善을 이해하고 실천할 意志가 없으면 사랑과 평화 행복과

번영의 조화도 실현될 수 없다는 嚴威한 비의(heavenly secret)가 지금까지 내 작품 전체에 훙건히 녹아있는 작품들이다.

예컨대 졸시 「추억」의 "주린 배 채운 하늘/타는 목 축인 별빛"에서 "배가 고픈데 하늘로 채운다거나, 목이 타는데 별빛으로 축인다."는 형상화의 이미저리는 일반적인 비유와 상징의 관념을 넘어 "상응"의 원리에 뿌리를 두고 있음이다. 시가 세상 밖으로 나가는 순간부터는 독자의 몫이란 걸 누가 모르겠는가? 그래도 아는 사람이 있어 가끔씩 가슴을 울리며 눈물이 핑 돌도록 떨리는 음성의 화답을 들을 수 있기에 부끄러움 무릅쓰고 시편들을 모아 세상 밖으로 내보낸다. 주인을 못 만나 떠도는 언어가 될지라도 …

감히, 데카르트의 신의 "존재증명"처럼, "나는 시를 쓴다. 고로 존재한다!"고 혼잣말을 하면서…

Contents

Ⅱ. Even the Small Bird Can Fly in the Sky_45

Ⅲ. The Shadow of Civilization_73

Ⅳ. When Shall the Day Come?_105

목차

Ⅱ부. 새는 작아도 하늘을 난다_159

Ⅲ부. 문명의 그늘_183

Ⅳ부. 그날은 언젠가?_209

I

Creating Poems

Creating Poems

The mind of writing a poem
Means still to survive,
The mind of composing a poem
Means to breathe more deeply,
This means so to lead a life
As a spider weave a web,
And as an ant builds his ant-hill.
Being distressed, a poem is to be conceived,
Being sad, a poem is to be vomited.
Being delighted, I enjoy the poem alone,
reciting it.

The Raving Winter Passed

At last it has come,
The bright and fresh spring
Vindicating the smart, tingly and wild winter!

The sunbeams like a flowery fire,
Burning up hot and hot are broken into pieces,
Look at there the glaring mountains and fields.

Shaking off, shaking off the old,
And taking off the winter tattered cloths,
Let' s change into the new-fresh clothes!

The larks chirp in the blue sky,
The brooks' s waters stream singing too,
With a gentle wind caressing the frozen swelling earth,

Rush to the green field singing,
And climb the high mountain singing,
Winter always comes and goes in such a manner.

For the Greater Happiness

The mind to throw away all things
The mind to leave all things,

Finally is the way we go alone,
Finally has nothing,

And,
And
The heaven, the wind, the wood, the star, the dream,
The vast land, the passion as the sunray, the innocence as lily,
And singing the song of hope----,

The discontent is poison,
The gratitude is good medicine,
The hatred is homicide,
The forgiveness is peace,
The honesty is sure victory,
Finally the love is life.

Another Departure. I

Can I complete the course?
Allowed life again
Racing in 365 days
Never short course.

Should have to win
When take away last calenda.
With same an oath
Only a firm promise being in my heart.
That' s a moment.
The last month of year is the same
From the equal loss despondency
Just blame for myself.

What can' t be helped
Abandonment will never speak yet.
Darkness prepare for dawn
Regret is triggering device

Of another challenge.
Over and over again
Should be to stand
On new point of departure.

From the Turning Point

– Certification of Being. 19

The field way,
Far-off and near,

Going across a thin ice river,
Passing over a thorny mountain,

Scattering the keenly tears,
Being pressed with the starved wild animal,

It's the path looking ahead to the future,
Not knowing of the rest journey,

Bud out as scattering and planting seeds?
Flower's fragrance and fruits abundant?

Unawares, it's the gloaming sunset to return
And it's my way to go as dreaming and sleeping.

Dawn's Path. 2

The wind, driving out darkness,
From where does it blow?
The watchman's night grows still late,

I walk alone the unknown path of dream
As going into the jungle.
Still the birds walk with a careful step
On the untrodden way of the beginning of the world.

Before long, day breaks, cloud and fog are cleared off,
Walking upright with the brilliant sunbeams embraced in my bosom,
The high and blue sky naturally comes in sight,
And the sound of my step is heard loudly.

The way of people losing hometown is far away,
And the way without hometown is wretched.
The way going to hometown is dawn's path.
The dawn's path is a holy way,
And the dawn's path, a solitary way.
That's my way I should go.

The Sandy Phenomena

Now
A visual field is zero,
An untimely gate-crasher,

Though it' s time dawn will come,
Though it' s time new spring will come,
Darkness that cannot draw back,
Bitter cold that cannot step aside,

That we fear and dread,
Is the trashes pined at one street of Yeoedo,
Those things not to be separated and removed,
And not to use the regular envelopes, are threw away,
Piled up, pushed here and there, entangled,
We are afraid of the nasty smell and the cold front to chase after,

And on-the-spot heavy fall, hails, and the loss of the farm products.

The sandy wind on April
We cannot open eyes with our eyeballs being rough,
And sands are chewed teasingly in our mouths,
So we wish the south wind to blow and the spring rain to fall down.

A Skylark. 2

There was a boy running in his bare feet
Along with a skylark in the lone mountain where a cuckoo
Disturbed loneliness
It was the road of yellow soil scattering the powder of pine flowers

The boy rushed into the glow of the setting sun
After running around,
Thinking that he could see something
If he had climbed the ridge of a mountain where a chickweed and
A violet came out splendidly
Or met the skylark

I wonder that the boy who burnt himself out becomes

A skylark
Now, sad news happens again and again
Between the sky and the Earth everyday
And cuckoo also spends its days in tears

After waiting a skylark
On the ridge of a mountain where the sun sets
One looks the sky whose eyes and ears are utterly worn out
And he doesn't know go away

A Gold Beetle's Nostalgia

Although its head get twisted
Just Tis the beetle
Makes the wind
Also let fly the body
Let him seek for the spot

Buzz Buzz Though the ill shoulder blade
Crosses the azure sky
Toward the dense ramie-shadow
He has to seek for the spot

Although cuts off the ankle
just Tis the beetle
With the wings can't fly
Whatever by the knees crawl
struggling let him fly away the spot

On the floor of verandah spin round
though his back's on fire
In the distance the horizon seen over
The bush clovers rank woods densely
He has to fly

Can he see whence
The soil and grass smelling beech
Can he find whence
The glaring wild-flower of the lost days

Here, the desolate plain
On the suffocated asphalt earth's crust

At the Station to Transfer. 3

Somewhere again
We should prepare to leave for.

When the short sun of the December
Declines to a daily calendar of the last month,
The platform of the snowy temporary station,
Not a terminal station,
Not a starting station,
But another station of destiny to transfer,
If the signal is given,
The new train enters proudly,

But the endless way however we may walk and walk,
It' s the way of a gypsy,
The unknown earth
And a harbour of our desire

Are the way passing by a mountain path, a waterway, and a desert way
To the plateau and the perpetual snow.

However, here,
Is a land of iron wall
Before the stopped rust train,
And it's a dark and gloomy station to transfer
Even a discolored dream withering in an old diary
Which has no freedom returning to our native town.

If I had Such a Friend

If I had such a friend
To me,

Talking with him about the flower's story all day long,
Without being tedious,
Then even in night,
Shifting the conversation to talk night away on the star's story,

Talking amiably on the star's story all through night,
And again changing the subject
As a long, long story on the music without end,

Talking the music story again,
Though the sun sets again,

If I had such a friend
As we could sing together
The flower's song,
The star's song,

How could my heart
Be delightful as floating lightly---?

A Certain Contradiction

– Certification for being. 25

Looking at the far mountain,
We bump against the rocks and break open,

Looking down onto only the chin's tip,
We tumble down over a stone,

Being unaware of life order of an erect standing pedestrian,
And more over, we couldn't see the wood and mountain together,

Unrealizing to degrade as a animal,
This global town is becoming as a cruel wild animal.

The middle sky's sun, suspended over the western hill,
Civilization grows dark with long black

shadow hanging down.

Darkness swallows light,
Light spoils darkness,

Here is only thesis and anti-thesis,
It's a land of chaos without synthesis.

The Crowing Sounds of Cock at Dawn

For all the world, we are unable to bear the sight
Of that lamentation on that day's dawn,

It's the worst tragedy for gaining 30 pieces of silver coins,

Today, tearing such chaos at dawn
And the darkish solitude as that night,

Hear the outcrying warning, "wake up, wake up, and wake up!"
Every dawn so as to be bruised at its syrinxes of the cock!

For all the life, I cannot make a sleep at dawn,
My own self, not being a king and a minister,

By chance being born in this world, living the lost 70 years,
Now the voice of *Fichte's speech has been heard every dawn,

How could we do if we have to send for 70 years, again 70th 70,
Just as we have the dividing barrier---?

* Fichte: he is a famous philosopher of Germany and for his speech, 'I inform our people of Germany'.

The Reason Why We Feel Heavy in Bosom

—Certification for Being. 4

There is sure to be a way
We are either shot up in the circumference of a circle,
Or are confined in the jail of four sides,
Or to all directions, to the infinite series---
There is sure to be a way. Only
A man's way and that of animal are different each other,
And there are a land route, a sea route, and an air one,
Only there are an earthly way and a heavenly one,
If we see only our finger and don't see the moon, the moon is not there,
But we can cross the waving sea by the tempest on food if know the way,
And if not, it would be an elephant before the blind.

The snow is water, the ice water too, and steam and could are water.

We are out of breath. So it' s so stuffy,
That it' s not water even looking at the water,
So our chest is about to burst out. The people, blocking up the river
are poor and same amaurotic persons who don' t
know the principle
That water doesn' t allow a wall and any iron wall too.
And the poor people, trying to block up such water that overflows out
Soaking into soil and ascends as clouds, again going down,
Until they are drowned, whether they don' t know water is way, truth, and life---.

The Wandering Language. I

Suddenly I see the wandering language
Filling up the heaven.
The pretty language like the white crane,
Which shot up at random,
Calls the master
With not to become the crane.

The people in the heaven can fathom into
The other people's mind by only their eye colors,
But only by their pretty adornment
Nobody can rejoice to see us
Wherever we may go,
And they can know even the hoodwinking intentions.

What we get along in this world
Is not an easy matter,

By what can we take a good aim
At the weight of the language
That is varying from season to season?

Because of the idle pledges
That will be a discolored festival before long,
The day, having a false sense of satiety foe a little while
And having a queasy feeling,

Looking at the river shallow,
Hearing 'the sailor' s song of Venezia'
We see the crows
Falling down, one by one.

II

Even the Small Bird Can Fly in the Sky

Even the Small Bird Can Fly in the Sky

In the bosom of poet
Birds sing
Birds sing through out the
spring, summer, autumn, winter

No, it is not cry
It's a chorus and oratorio that carry
The peace of heaven which
We can hear in the bush

As soon as the aria of angels finished
A gust of outcry
Oh, no just listen to the endless outcry
With breathless attention

'A mad man, mad men
When the day breaks,
We fetch peace from the heaven

Bur those men will abruptly demolish it

Please listen to the song
In a modest way
'Useless, useless'
It is sad song in pitiable condition

'Get along well today
For the love of God, don' t take place
The collapse of heaven!'
Mountains sound as echoes
Fields also sing in the wind

Even the small bird can fly in the sky.

Looking at the Winter's Trees

– Certification for Being. 1

Behold the birds' elegy and poem for condolence,
And a requiem tolling on the gaunt branches,
The trees get over so through the winter.

The nihility and mutability of the gigantic trees
Soaring up to the sky, scattering lots of last letter of will
That has no place to go on the paved street and field,
And that has torn trembling, shaking, sprinkling,

Only animal's wild raving in the field of reeds,
Being cruel in the salt pond evaporated with human nature and tears,
There finding no place to stay, like a hunger

wild goose,
Pawing the air endlessly as an albatross
Between clouds and the blur moonlight,
I continue to fly on yesterday, today, and tomorrow,

O, the brilliant sun, the burning sun's rays, the sunlight,
Shine this dark cave so as to be dazzling,
Even though shrunk, distorted as that winter trees,
Shine again as a original life reviving on tomorrow!

A Little Happiness

The night
Where the stars of even size bloom as the fog flowers,
And the winds, swaying,
Soothe the dew-laden grass leaves.

Not getting a sleep
In feeling the lack without reason,
Through the window where dawn brightens
A falling star falls
As another life falls,
Suddenly, I hear one sound
From the end of my pillow I slept crying.

Only one,
To a man who could not be robbed of more things,
That is just a tear like a dawn's dewdrop

Witch no one could take away more.

This
Is my happiness,
That is a clear dewdrop
Leading to the heaven.

A Computer Out of Order

– Certification for being. 2

For all my pains with a computer out of order,
I sat up all long night of December.

Even beating, touching, and pattering it,
To the last I didn't my object.

A rooster flapping the wings, crowed
As the heartless voice of metal things of the computer with no soul.

A senseless, foolish life would be better for me
Than the arrogant scientist without paradise.

5. Duty

– Certification for Being. 6

Duty is a flower of life,
The flower of the flowers is the flower of life like a field flower..
Obeying the law is a solid fruit and the highest good,
If the flower blooms, the world becomes all the flower gardens.
Birds bees, and butterflies dance and sing together,
Advancing breath with fragrances of lily, lilac, amaranth, and orange,
This global towns where the harmonious peace overflows are all paradises,
Every person will yearn for the day on blooming such flowers at every places.

The world without flowers is the dark ruins,
The dark dugout haunting with goblins on

days,
A dreadful, lonely, and grieved heart like a desert,
The Gobi desert where humanity and tears dried up,
And the shadeless, far, far land of the palm-tree near oasis.

They are the falling beings without names and being's marks,
And so pitiful as big iris field-flower buried under a heavy snowfall.
O! the flower's fragrance like holy hands of an ascetic Buddhist monk
The brown stars falling and dazzling at the night-sky.

A Long Drought
– Certification for Being. 3

The thirsty shouting touches the heaven,
We spoil farming for children to go down.

The leaping, respiring things in the mountains, fields, and rivers,
The heaven and earth shakes in soundless wriggle.
Where did all officials for anti-flood and afforestation go?
They are all indifferent and so always carrying out their duty,
And the resounding echo is---(Stop making us laugh, who are we?---)
Where we impeach no business in opening stores,
No wage for no labor?

O, the careless heaven and the earth, now

that's
enough,
Please relieve rages for homicides of this land!
For the land of embroidered rivers and mountains,
and its peoples at the corner in the global world,
Let us realize water is the very life, and give us a fire extinguisher
To control uranium and plutonium!

Impersonality
– Certification for Being. 8

I am not a man yet.
Though solely I am nervous for being a man,
I've no way to solve it easily and sit up painfully all night.
Calling upon the big bookstores repeatedly,
And looking for the rough lumbers, to trim them, shave them,
And to build them, I have no one house to live in,
I am not a man yet. Moreover I cannot throw an objective light
On my personal history and on what I was,
Now only I am pawing the air to get out the dilemmas,
How can I say a man? Much more is it the case with a great poet.
Though having well balanced features,
I didn't help the unhappy people to wipe

their painful tears out,
Now not giving an armful of happiness to them,
And not elucidating life system of the universe and l' reason de etre,
When would I become a poet like a man?
When should I become a man like a poet?
O, man! people like a dog and beast!

The Bat-Blind Persons

Being torn,
Being broken,
And being scratched,
A shape, being rooted out,
How can we lay the blame only on the rain and wind?

Out minds
Are torn to pieces,
Are broken,
And are scratched,
So this global town shaking even to their roots.

The slaves of a fetishism
Who are deaf and blind to the strict aphorism
About the dark shadows of the civilization suspended thickly,

And who are not to pay attention to it,

Where is the last stop of the sneaking beasts
at the field of reeds
Without blood and tear?
That arrogant waves, crowded like the fearful,
terrible reeds being empty,
The great power rushing like the surge,
And the suffocating war of the stars----,

When did we lost our Eden Garden at the
beginning of the world?
A crowd of people, expanding a great
desolate desert
by the internet equipped on every thing
Instead of the place of man's heart, mind,
soul, spirit, and creativity!

At the Platform of the Subway

That is not an electric railcar,
It's a pelagic-fishing vessel blowing its siren
And I am a fledgling fisherman within.

Though the vessel moves forward,
facing with lots of critical problems, shaking,
tearing,
And colliding with its rolling and pitching,
Only we all beg God's help for safer return
and getting a good catch,

Even if our pains are changed into pebble-
stones and sands
At the critical moment like a war of death,
They should be formed as a brilliant pearl and
ruby---.

A Night View of the Han River

The light flows
On the river.

Nothingness is piled up
On the beyond shore where the civilization flows,

Though the starlights pour out,
The recollection of the people's losing their home-town is sad,

The blue mercury lamp-light from afar,
Also gives a surprise to my heart as if it were a national border.

The striking sound,
Or something like overflowing wine glasses,

Is the sound that the Tower of Babel is tumbling down
As a deep earthshaking rumble.

At the Window Dawn Opens

When a small ship running the Milky Way
through night,
Drops the anchor
Upon the ridge of the western hill
As the numbed eyes to this world,

Someone embraces the mother earth
As his endless love,
The footmark' s sounds are heard,
Pushing darkness and getting up.

If darkness is ruminated,
Silver-grey resurrection would be born,
Then something is reversed itself again
As a melancholic chaos,

If we listen to
The window where dawn opens,

The crowing sounds of the cock on the last day,
And the deep breath of the disciple named Peter, seem to be heard,
Why here at dawn,
From a small corner spinning round in 4 Kalpa,
The cuckoo bird could be choked with sorrow,
And why the falling star could sink over the mountain?

A Window Facing the South

I am living
On a window facing the south.

All through the night,
Wandering into darkness
If I greet the break of dawn
As the tired soul,
Always I' ve a soaking lamplight,
Today my soul is animated.

Leaning my mind on the little window
Facing the south,
Heaven opens in blue color,
White clouds swelling up
The breath of life is opened,
Come to the end of the heaven.

If I hadn' t a little window facing the south,
How could I keep on living?

A Landscape of my Native Place

Turning around the earthen wall
The stable of a boiled cattle fodder appears,

A drawing room's lamp between the brushwood door
Of trifoliate orange tree flows out,

Today the soft voices, waving hands
Waving hands and calling,

Hit the wayfarer's ears
Who was tired in wandering.

A Violet

Her shy erotic mind
Not attracting her eyes
To a man being in a flurry,
With having so mystic legends
As brilliant,
Seeking for a deserted place down
She whispers in another' s ear
Sparkling as the stars.

'With all her life,
The world
Is so much boisterous' ,
Pouring out, 'she pines for such old friends
As a broad-leaved plantain, a stonecrop, and
a lettuce greens' ---,
She, a song,
And an innocence like fragrance!

Is she waking up our minds being sick
In urban city disease like asphalt?---
Splitting open the asphalt and bricks,
And singing a lost pastoral,
Swaying her slender head
With a soft wind.

The Grass Flower Blooming in the Snow

– Certification for Being. 18

As soon as I see a petal of the field flower
Budding out from chinks of melted snow in no time,
I am frightened as getting shocked by electricity.

Being sick with inflammation of the liver, and nervous gastritis,
The grass flower I encounter on the hill beside a lake into deep mountain,
The grass is not weeds, but one of the medical herbs God gave me.

Asking about the grass flower here and there what it is,
I knew it in a pictorial book of Korean flora,
its name is "Veronica Persica"
Which is kept beside my sickroom with its

branch cutting,

As making incantation through all day,
I fell in love conversing with it,
For a new life to flow in.

At last I reject 'the god of death'
With whom Pyeonjak could not cope,
Even now I've walked on snow-path looking
for the grass flower.

III

The Shadow of Civilization

The Shadow of Civilization

1. A Condolence on the Limpid Little Snail's Death

O, it's sad, today!
Unexpectedly born as a trifling thing to live in man's society,
Leaving behind you, the native place
With shade of green-colored trees and the river,
And your parents and brothers who you want to see awfully!

The life's order of the universe,
That is, one of the global town,
Whatever the alive things are,
They are worth to exist in the world,
Together, also worth to live with,
The global families estranged from modern civilization,
Before the righteous governing of the arrogance

So called 'Man is the Lord of all creation'
In the world of 'the Law of Jungle' depriving the right to live,
Forgive our sins(faults)
Not to prepare for your environment for existence,
And good bye!
And have a good sleep, you, little transparent snails!

A Shade of Civilization

2. An Epitaph of the Little Limpid Snail

Here under the shade of a magnolia,
At the sunny spot
A rose, a narcissus, a peony blossom, and a canna flower
Bloom and fade by turns,
The little pellucid snail slept silently forever without a native place.

In the beginning,
According to the Creator's will,
The little limpid snail lives together with us in the world.
You and I
Are going around the dark place of the civilization
Under the pretense of the mask,
And our body and mind are showing a right way

Which is fairness and justice of life,

When rain comes, exposing to rain,
The wind blows, exposing to wind,
Without a granary, and a storehouse,
Flung a suit of pellucid clothes on as it has been,
And living without any faults through life,

Beside of the moonlit lake in night,
At the green field of the dazzling sun in days,
Breathing in the smell of the soil and the grass,
Drinking the sweet nectar from the grass,
And enjoying your happy life without any grudge,

Being pressed by the boom of development-promoted,
And poisoned by an insecticide sprayed carelessly,
So stanching the flow of blood,
Killing a nerve cell,

But not making a protest,
You have to be died lonesomely.

Therefore,
Making strictly precautions on the toxicity of civilization,
I am going to stop the end of global town,
All the people, passing by the little snail's epitaph
Humbly I beg them to have the limpid little snail's lesson
Engraved on their minds---.

A Whispering Language the Waves Conveyed

Extricating myself from a daily swamp
Pressed down so breathless,
And dropping a little anchor of my own life-ship
At a little island in the south sea
Then hearing the sounds of waves,
Ebbing and swelling without a rest
From this end of the sky to that end of the sky,
Suddenly I look over my shoulder at my sea route of life,
That the waves of my life,
Breaking to pieces, ducking, and rising up again.

Life is something like a piece of waves,
So we cannot stay on a spot in a while
All things are roaming from place to place.
Coming to an island, an island doesn't look like an island,

The land also is not much different from the island.
What I have seen and heard all things in the world,
Would be perhaps an optical illusion and hallucination.

There is nothing unshaken in the world,
In the same way, there is nothing not to flow.
The river flows,
The sea flows,
And a wind and clouds flow too,
Love and dream also stream, streaming,
How long could I stay here,
At this little island?

The coconut palm's shadow is cool,
The plantain's sleeves lead me into temptation sensually,
How long the small grapnel's cable could be fixed?
The winds
And the waves
To a certain degree, are benevolent?

At a Sandy Beach

Behold the process
A sheer cliff, rocks of the precipice,
Even the unknown reefs under the deep sea
Have been changed into sands like powder,

Behold their moving round freely as they please,
Being pushed by the typhoon,
And being torn by the waves,
At last the intrinsic shape vanishing to dust
Without being left a clue behind.

Behold
their instant extinction like clouds
Suspended on the white sands,
Without their own voices,
Without having their own colors
Only with the faded beings.

And behold again,
A lot of footmarks like the sands,
And submission piling up pushed by the
waves!

On An Excursion Ship at the Han River

– at 3rd night, the 24th World Poets Conference

To flow is not the river,
To flow is peace, love, the wave of a poem.
It's the wave of the poem flowing in the bigger sea
For all the people of all world to meet with one another.

That thing shining brightly outside the window is not a lamp,
But that, driving out darkness, is truth, wisdom,
And a light of the heaven to let our people live together,
And a burning flambeau to let us rekindle inside
Every, every hearts,

Also It's a beautiful flower light of our, our bosoms

To let us drive out wars, green envies, and jealousies.

To flow
Is not only the Han river,
To shine brightly
Is not only the fire-light of a night view of Seoul.

The Wandering Language. III

- Certification for being. 10

My loving poems, my souls!
Now, are you wandering, crying under any sky?

Passing the winter-night flying wild geese with honk at Bukcheon,
Or the mountain slope with a plot of mugwort on open fields,

Like the traveler of 'a wayfarer of winter',
With his head put in his coat's collar, and his guitar on his shoulder,

To the dark night's way for himself where the dogs bark wildly,
Do you wonder, singing a soul's song to the heaven lonely?

Without having no love, passion, a sweet

heart, a friend, a follower,
And with being utterly worn out, and falling
in music, blind in music,

To the house with a tender evening lamp and
artistic soul,
Running by a post wagon, and passing by
wood where crows are cawing,

Do you look for the spot to rest anxiously
without a milestone?
Or do you roam about blowing out for your
frozen hands?

O, so much for today, take a rest, with your
tears wiped out,
Rest at ease for finding a dream of spring, a
dream of spring,
My poems!

The Late Season's Rose

Toward the end of October,
And at closing this year
Where should the dry leaves go scattering about?

Keeping the sad spot under the foot of a mountain with glow,
And feeling somewhat sad at looks trembling, and shaking,
The wild goose also might have soared up honking a long honk
Over the sky of a blue cold moonlight.

Taking down her splendid crown as a deposed queen,
Refusing his gorgeous glory as a prince,
Being touched with its poor and ephemeral migration,

Even the cricket might have chirped as a tearful poem
Getting the cold frost in the grasses' wood.

If the warm winds blow on the hill of the sun again,
Should the double pedaled brilliant flower pedals bloom?
And should they the ecstatic fragrance spread out again?

An Ecstatic Elegy

1. A Solitary National Ship

Ah, the brilliant light of history
Now, is it going to die away?
The clouds of the dark hardship,
How long shall they throw over us?
The Korea is a lamp of the orient,
With long, long history, that is called, 'the degraded confidence'
Is hung our head for shame.
Our lofty spirit like a mountain,
Is it going to disappear as an empty dream?

Ah, this dangerous route of a passage!
The boundless expanse of water with surging waves!
A solitary national ship
Is rocking dangerously,
Wake up racial souls!

A lamp of this age!
Look at the cold eyes
An which the world gazes carefully.
Let's make our brilliant history
Shine once more.

A Certain Evolution
– Certification for Being. 7

The sparks in our heads give out a flash.
Pest, Aids, Ebola, Cholera, Mers---
It's the unforseen dreadful war of enemies.

The slaves of fetishism devoting themselves to the endless repetition
For oblivion of beings with Nobel's will,
Will aid and abet the wicked breeding at being at a loss
Today, tomorrow, and the next day.

Pay your attention to an epigram, 'to aid the wicked breeding
Means an ugly thing handing many enemies over your offsprings,
And we have to stop up the breeding of the weak
In order to survive the fit persons!

Litmus Paper
– Certification for Being. 11

In sorrow, tears come to my eyes,
In joy, laughter bursts out again and again,
Being unpleasant, I lose my temper,
Getting better, soon I become to be a child.
So I will take medicine of a sedative.

The blue color means the sky, the red color the
sun,
Light and impurity, truth and a falsehood,
How can I judge by only two colors
The life's order of the universe?
Really I will take a sedative.

Soaring Up to the Heaven Again. 4

Soar up to the azure heaven again clapping her wings,
Like a lark and an albatross!

You, pressed with intense heat, typhoon, the torrential rain,
And a tidal wave, the white-clad angels, who have lost the place
To go and rest at a chaotic wood being twisted, torn, and crumpled!

The heavenly passage, blocked up by the stubbornly commotion
And the pent-up barrier for 70 years, how could we do to help,
"That we aid and care for increasing their wicked things
Of the north people is like a foul thing

handing over lots of enemies to our offspring."

You like the wild animals at the reed's field, being blinded and deaf
By the gold and power, falsehood and trick, and in spite of a pretext Like things sorrowful, tearful, and resentful, you have no place
To hide even in your gorgeous villa, now have to fade away in this world!
Hearing an ejaculation knocking and hanging on the national ship
Every day and dawn in auditory hallucination, I am praying.

Now slender barley's ears, revived through the frozen land
Are waving as a new life at spring season, and the larks sings
The sky without a magnolia, you like wild animals,
Drinking a gold cup in the wide green field like abode of demons,

Are you going to live such a cruel life as that of March, April, May,
and June?

It's Not To be Haste

Could we wait in slackening one step,
After taking deep breaths looking at the sky a moment?

Even a little conciliatory attitude
Helps to reject unexpected disasters,

Our haste mind, don't break into the queue,
And keep it in mind through life!

Hurrying up one day like one thousand days,
Who knows to lose all things at the moment?

So we cannot count the true happiness and peace
With a hand of second.

To a Poet

A poet,
Your eyes are a bolt of lightning,
A terrible lightning,
Realizing all universe through its purpose
In a moment.

Your head is a knife,
As the King Solomon judged the last judgment,
It is a knife like a cold flash
Which can cut off the head at one stroke.

Your mind is a sun,
That is a fireball burning
As love of 8, or 9 thousand degrees,
So is called a melting furnace
Which could melt the cast iron, the stone, and even filthy ice.

Your breast is a small spring
Like mother's bosom,
Always gushing out soft life-giving water,
The way farers
Rest peacefully,
And a fountain of life overflowing
On our way returning home.

Your respiration is a chorus,
As a cantata or toccata pouring out
With a holy and pure delight,
That is a bell-sound waking the hell'
s sleeping.

You are a tired pregnant woman,
Who should be careful in eating, putting on
clothes, sleeping,
And in bringing up a life in her womb for 300
days,
That means a pregnant woman,
Suffering from losing her taste for food.

Now you are a lighthouse,

That is shining without a break
Through all dark night
Rising uprightly in the midst of a boundless sea
Not having the 7 stars of the Big Dipper.

At last you become a bugler,
Ringing a mountain and a field,
And a poet! who should blow a bugle to the full
Until returning as an echo of the end of heaven
Over the horizon.

54. Ch' oso*

The wind blowing in the field of soybeans
Cooled the heat of the earth all too soon

Birds in the fields of sorghum
Fly away busily

Loved things of mindless like wind
And things of changes like cloud

Whispering something
With all its might

Leaving behind things of nostalgic sweetness,
Things that sunk deep in one' s mid

So, it is like summer
That glides by heartlessly

The yearning is washed away by the waves
Even if the scorching heart tried to flow as a river

The yearning is shaken violently
Even if it tried to be rock to forget

It's the sad droning of cicadas in the woods
And it's a serenade yelling into my ear

* one of the 24 seasonal divisions of around August 23rd.

Yearning

O!, o, where did my love go?
Without a word,
When I see you from afar,
It is more than I can bear
That yearning at the sunset
Is as high as the waves.

If you go off with the high and deep affection left behind,
How can I do?
If you want to leave for sure,
Even you have gone together with my mind,
It would be better to do so,
Rather such a mind makes me more painful than death.

The man I am longing for,
Where are you under any heaven?

Only empty heaven and drifting clouds
Are lonesome on the wind,
This evening's loneliness makes me sad
At every time pining for you.

IV

When Shall the Day Come?

When Shall the Day Come?

Looking around Jungfrau, altitude of 3454 meters,
And absorbed in the perpetual snow's peak,
Its name where a virgin and a peak met, the ice tracking,
A walking path on the snow, a Sphinx Terrace, and an Ice-Palace,
But a sudden idea of the crater lake on Mt. Baek-Du
Flashes across my mind, and on

The holy mountain's lake with the open hot spring,
And Mt. Diamond mountain that we could have been to,
Keeping people away with iron fence for over 70 years,
Besides, the northern people have digged

caves madly like moles
Day and night, making nuclear bombs and trying to test,
Answer us! When are you going to pay your attention?

Uranium and Plutonium are only materials leading to the hell's gate,
Don't you know it really? it's a vagrant fancy of all destruction,
And a ghost image like a movie. Now taking off your dark mask of a ghost,
Riding on the cows like the day we regain the land which had been lost,
And like the day playing the Korean music and weaving through the golden field.
Let's sing a real song of the restoration of independence, and hurrah for our unification.

If the day comes, so our all Korea opened as one way,
And if the dam-water of peace flows out from Mt. Hanra, to Mt. Bark-Du,

How we feel envy of Jungfrau and a permanent
neutral state?
Answer us, the scientists and politicians, and
the millionaires!
When could we restore our true soul of the
White Clad Race?

Time Out

When, who, at any season,
Could the day to whistle come to us?
At the moment the iron sound touches,
As the sun and the intense heat are burning to vanish away,
Prior to the war of the stars happens,
Could we find a referee to whistle, sentencing "Time Out"
To the wild beasts in the reeds field and the powerful men
Enjoying the law of jungle, and abusing their rationality and free-will?

The inversion of 'the black and the white' and 'the good and the vice',
Being magnified and reproduced by its vicious cycle,
Leads us to make peace into war, harmony

into discord,
Happiness into infelicity, prosperity into defeat,
Freedom into debauchery, and variety into confusion, that is to say,
The sneaking intelligent highbrows like all out-side show men!
The ignorant and the poor have been unparalleled, really not
In the records of the world history that they provoked the war---,

Science calls forth the big wars between the stars,
Politics only has high jinks for his own interests,
And even up to the sudden richers by any means
Are swarmed like maggots in the open rest room
By means of the crowded force as empty as reeds,
And of the wicked paradox to let this world

bring to ruin,
Then the wandering aliens with standing no more,
Ye have lost the spot to go! Our lost paradise,

When, where could we find it?
They say, the living creature on the Jupiter hang around
Because they couldn't approach near this earth, the global town
In which the human beings emit offensive smells polluted by them---,

The judge, the fair judge! "please, whistle against the vicious cheating game to end it."
Before this global town is spoiled all to pollute other stars,
Before the gloomy shade of civilization swoops upon us heavily!

Another Departure. 2

Again somewhere
Is there a new starting line?
The year and the season changed,
But I've no place to go. Looking back,
I've only the turning point like a critical moment,
It's heartbreaking, but how can I? The seniors like bugs
Who have no place to trust and depend on, and have evil news,
And praying to God before going to bed, after sleeping and waking up,
Running a new morning with two clenched fists,
But now only gestures of non gravitation running through empty space like feather,
The seeding in the wintry rain, sprouting new buds

From every green, lightly barley leaf after harvest,
Gives comfort to them going for an uphill pass of the absolute solitude.

To wait for the starting line seems to be a bless to them.
The starting line of days ebbing and flowing like flood tide
As if they go up and down the subway, the bus, the crossway,
And the footbridge's entrance, gasping, gasping for breath,
There, at the starting line, is there a place to stand up now?

The House I Design

I will build a little house
Of which window faces to the east.

Opening the window,
Always this is the place
Where the mountain and the sea come into view.

In the night the stars came down,
Leave the stories of a far home town loosened,
In the day, the mountain winds passed,
This is the place which is opened stopped bosoms.

Without autumn, spring, and summer,
The field flowers embrace their limpid sunlight,
Which is the place
That they are swaying and giving a deep bow.

I

Will build my own eternal house.

This is the spot where the sound of the water, the wind,

The bird, and the insect

Are living together

Without fences.

Autumn

The place
Where wind swept away
The shadow of hardtime is
Grief

It rains
Late in autumn
A wild bird in the field of reeds
Flutters its wings
it' s the bird that lost
It' s way

From a distance hill
The evening dusk is
Gathering

Living and Repenting

Living, repenting, I write poems.
Sometimes standing on the desolate waste land,
Being tired in hot heat
Without one shot sudden shower,
Or taking pains, I have walked on the icy road.

The setting sun, the rising moon
When did I have a chance to look at them once?
Getting pursued and running after, I have lived looking ahead to the future

O, it' s far-off, looking back at my path,
Every way I' ve walked
Is covered with pains and tears forming dews,
When a wind blows,
I see it would carry us to earth transitorily.

If we pass over one hill,
At that time all experiences
would be delight or sadness.

The Wayfarers

We are the wayfarers,
After we slept,
Again the destiny we are bound depart for,

To the mountains and the fields
Passing over crossroad,
The fate we bound to follow the signals,

The mountains to pass over,
The rivers to cross over,
So, today and tomorrow,

Where can we meet
The wayfarers to go with
Though the dark road at night?

The Window

Chewing the cud of loneliness
Invites the straight there

Lying sidelong in longing
One watches moonlight leak in there

The pain of dream deprived of
And the hurt of disheartenment

The wind outside brushes past and takes care of
And the cloud up there passes by and gives comfort to

The weary spirit, weakened from hunger
During his journey, takes rest, watching the heavens

Though the walls, rising higher day
By day, stand in the way of humanity

One, his neck lengthened, looks up just at
The far mountain, longing for his home.

The Native Village

A dog's barking
from a far village
resounds the ribs of lattice door
The flickering
fire of small horong lamp
These are of a gray-haired
man's native village he recalls from his
memory

On the evening when large
snowflakes are falling thick
and fast he sees
his married-away sister's
feet-tracks printed on the soy-jar terrace

These are the shadow of
his native village coming to his mind
all of a sudden from nowhere, making him

awaken

And it is
a moon night
When he misses his home
under falling moonlight

And it is
a moon night
When he misses his home
under falling moonlight
By day, stand in the way of humanity

One, his neck lengthened, looks up just at
The far mountain, longing for his home.

Looking at the Woods. 5

I see the woods be covered by the darkness again,
And hear pathos
With a sound carried on the soft wind.

The ruins, being unable to the sight for all the world,
To the Trade Center across the sea, the buildings' wood of the Pentagon,
On the day of the 21 century Babel Tower's shape,
Before the blackish red dragon's raving of Poseidon and Hurricane,
If I

Consecrate a song of the Requiem,
'Pieta Signore!' *
Could the scratch by the typhoon be healed?

The people of the wood's country are crying in their disheveled hairs,
Writhing in flowing blood, and even the rocks, shaking at every room
Where the coffins were placed,

Now, no more, the Wind!,
As tearing even the great mountain's waist into pieces,
It's so tedious,
The crazing wind,
Being ceaseless, insane wind!
And if it happens again, a rumor, panic-stricken rumors
Make a rush for us like black clouds to cast over,
The woods are covered with darkness again,
The world is for us not to hear the mystical legend
With even the stars' light veiled.

* It's a sacred song by A. Stradella.

Cultivating Spring
– Certification for Being. 23

A wild plain, seen all the more they go into the wood,
Those old days, plowing a rice paddy and rows of a field driving a cow,
How much I pine for them!

If we lose the chance for spring plowing,
The spring season passes like a thief,
Soon presses on us the snowfall of cold winter like a robber,
Who shall fill up, and with what fill up the empty stomach of that day
And the storeroom full of coldness?

The fallow fields that the machinery's sound was clamorous,
And thistles and thorn bushes at this spring
Might screen the sky thickly?

That is, 'whatever we sow, we gather in as it is.'

Now, if we don't turn over the ground and select side splits,
And if we don't sow the seed of blood, sweat, and the true tears,
There is nothing to have it forever in the world
That we could fill up the empty storehouse.

A Song of Seeding

I' m a farmer planting seed
In an alien mountains and streams of
A secluded place

I' m lonely but blessed one,
Rooting and picking up
A thorny bush and a gravelly field, and
Sowing good seeds

When a spring breeze blows in cool ripples,
Flowers sway buoyantly in the air
When mountain birds sing merrily,
A stream murmurs along

To make the world beautiful
All together,
Offering a fervent prayer
For the yields in thirty, sixty, one hundred times

A Cup of Coffee

If one puts a cup of coffee,
Our minds are closely
Connected with each other
And love is also the same way

If one is not able to drink
A cup of strong coffee
It is really a matter for regret

On the day when I don't share coffee
With someone
It is always as bitter as gall

We, of course, should live,
Sharing the bitters of glass.

A Dreamy Sound

– At Ariul*

O, a dreamy sound ....,
Falling on my ear
It' s lapping sound of waves
All night through,
Coming from the horizon in the distance,
For which is transforming into the land
The sound of conceiving a new life
The sound of the waves with golden colors,
Beating upon the seashore
The sound of peace and prosperity
Approaching in a surging mass

O, it' s coming ...., the dreamy sound
Here, on the Land of Morning Calm
The sound whispering all day long
Beyond the horizon in the distance
The sound of giving birth to s new life
O, it' s the sound pulsating on the silver waves

One after another
The sound of flaring up - the lamp of the east

O, it falls on my ear ...., the dreamy sound
It's coming from the place
Beyond the vast and clear sea,
On which all the people the world
Will live all together
It's the sprouting sound of a new civilization
It's the sound of setting our cares aside
It's just the sound,
Blooming into only love for humanity
O, o.... the sky, the earth, the seaway

* 'Ariul' is a compound or a newly-coined word . The word is a synonym for the land reclamation program project for the 'Saomangcum' which is one of the national projects.

As civilizations were born along the banks of the Nile, this place is also in the hope of evolving into a new paradigm birthplace of altruistic thought as the lamp of the east.

A Retrospection

The sky that filled his hunger
Starlight that moist his thirst

When poverty passed by
It becomes a handful of memory

A wind passing by an old pine
Is blowing all over the heavens

The wings torn by typhoon
Will be rest on the shore of lake

I

시작 詩作

시작詩作

시를 쓰는 마음은
아직 살아 있다는 것
시를 짓는 마음은
좀 더 깊이 숨 쉬고 싶다는 것
거미가 실을 뽑아내듯
개미가 집을 짓듯
그렇게 살아가는 것
괴로울 때 시를 잉태하고
슬플 땐 시를 토해내고
기쁠 땐 혼자 읊조리며 즐기느니.

그 광란의 겨울은 가고

마침내 오고야마는구나！
쓰리고 아렸던 모진 겨울
설욕하는 화창한 새봄이

뜨겁게, 뜨겁게 꽃불 타오르는
햇살 부서져 눈이 부신 저기
푸른 산 푸른 들판을 보아라.

털어버리고, 털어버리고
겨울 누더기 벗어버리고
하 푸른 새 옷을 갈아입자

종달새는 하늘에서 지저귀고
얼부푼 땅 애무하는 미풍에
시냇물도 노래하며 흐르나니

웃으면서 달려가자 푸른 들을
노래하며 올라보자 높은 산을
겨울은 항용 그리 오고 가나니

더 큰 행복을 위하여

모든 것을 버린다는 마음
모든 것을 떠난다는 마음

결국 홀로 가는 길이란 것을
결국 아무 것도 아니란 것을

그리고
그리고
하늘과 바람과 강과 숲과 별과 꿈과 광활한 대지와
햇살 같은 열정, 백합 같은 순결
소망의 노래를 부르는 것과...

불평은 독약
감사는 선약
증오는 살인
용서는 화평
정직은 필승
사랑은 곧 생명인 것을

또 다른 출발. I

완주할 수 있을까
다시 주어진
삼백 예순 다섯 날의
짧지 않은 코스를

결코 승리하고 말리라
마지막 달력을 뜯을 때면
언제나 같은 맹세로
내심 입술을 깨물지만,
그것도 잠시
훌쩍 선달이 되고나면
같은 상실과 허탈감으로
좁은 가슴만 쥐어뜯는다

어쩌겠는가 그래도
포기는 영원히 아니 될 말
어둠은 새벽을 불러오고
후회는 또 다른 도전의

기폭제가 되느니
몇 번이고 몇 번이고
새로운 출발선에
서 볼 일이다

반환점에서

– 존재증명. 19

멀고도 가까운
아스란 벌판길

살얼음 강을 건너
가시밭 산을 넘어

뼈아픈 눈물을 뿌리면서
굶주린 맹수에 쫓기면서

앞만 보고 달려 온 길인데
남은 여정 알 수도 없는데

뿌리고 심은 대로 나 있을까
꽃향기와 열매는 풍요로울까

어느새, 돌아갈 불타는 황혼녘
잠자듯 꿈꾸듯 가야할 나의 길

새벽길. 2

어둠을 몰아내는 바람은 어디서
불어올까 파수꾼의 밤은
깊기만 한데

밀림 속 거닐듯 미지의 꿈길을
혼자서 걸어간다. 아직 새들도
파닥이지 않는 태초의 동산 길을
발자국도 조심조심 걸어간다.

이윽고 먼동 트며 운무 걷힌 하늘
찬란한 빛살 가슴안고 직립보행하면
저절로 안중에 들어오는 높푸른 하늘
내 발자국소리도 크게 들려오는 것을

실향민의 길은 아스랗다
고향을 버린 길은 서질하다
고향으로 가는 길은 새벽길이다
새벽길은 거룩한 길
새벽길은 외로운 길
오늘도 가야할 나의 길

황사현상

지금
시계視界 제로zero
때 이른 불청객

새벽이 올 때도 되었건만
새봄이 올 때도 되었건만
물러갈 줄 모르는 흑암
물러갈 줄 모르는 혹한

두렵고 두려운 건
여의도 1번지에 쌓인 쓰레기
분리수거 규정봉투 안 쓴 것들
마구 버려 쌓이고 밀리고 뒤엉켜
몰고 올 악취와 한랭전선 그리고
쏟아질 지도 모를 국지성 호우와 우박
망쳐버릴 농작물 피해

눈망울 껄끄러워 뜰 수 없고

입안엔 지근지근 모래 씹히는
4월의 황사, 마파람에 봄비라도
주룩주룩 쏟아졌으면…

종달새. 2

송화 가루 흩날리는 황토 언덕길
뻐꾸기 혼자 적막을 깨는 공산空山
종달새 노래 따라 맨발로 달리던
소년이 있었네.

아기별꽃 제비꽃 흐드러진
산등성 오르면 보일 것 같아
종달새를 만나면 알 것 같아
정신없이 달리고 달리다가
서녘 하늘 타오르는 불길에
뛰어든 소년.

불타버린 소년은
종달새가 되었을까
땅과 하늘 사이엔 날마다
슬픈 일만 일어나고 있는데
뻐꾸기는 지금도 울고 있는데

종달새 기다리다
저무는 산등성
눈도 귀도 다 어두워진
하늘만 쳐다보며
떠날 줄을 모르네.

풍뎅이의 향수鄕愁

모가지가 비틀려도
풍뎅이는 풍뎅이지
바람을 일으켜서
일으켜서 몸뚱이를 날려서
찾아가야지

여윈 죽지로라도 윙윙
파아란 하늘 가로질러
우거진 모시밭 그늘
찾아가야지

발목이 잘려나도
풍뎅이는 풍뎅이지
날개로 못 날면
무릎으로 무릎으로라도
허우적허우적 날아가야지

툇마루바닥 맴돌다가

등바닥에 불이 나더라도
아스란 지평선 너머
싸리꽃 칡덩굴 우거진 숲속
날아가야지

어딜 가면 만날 수 있을까
흙냄새 풀냄새 파고드는 너도밤나무
어디 가면 찾을 수 있을까
잃어버린 날의 햇살부신 들꽃들

여기 황량한 벌판
숨 막히는 아스팔트 지각地殼에서

환승역. 3

어디론지 다시
떠날 채비를 해야겠다

섣달의 짧은 해가 마지막
달력의 끝장 속으로 지고 나면
눈 내리는 간이역 플랫폼
종착역도 아닌
시발역도 아닌
또 다른 운명의 환승역
시그널이 떨어지면
새로운 열차는 도도히 들어오지만

가도 가도 끝없는
집시의 길
미지의 대지
소원의 항구
산길 뱃길 사막을 지나 고원에서 만년설까지…

하지만 여긴,
멈춰버린 녹슨 객차 앞에
장벽이 내려진 땅, 퇴색한 꿈마저
묵은 일기장 속에서 사그라지는,
귀향의 자유조차 없는
어둡고 답답한 환승역

이런 친구 하나 있었으면

나에게
이런 친구 하나 있었으면

진종일 꽃 이야기 늘어놓아도
지루한 줄 모르는
그러다가 밤이 되면
별 이야기로 꽃 피우고,

오순도순 별 이야기로
밤이 새면 다시 긴긴
음악 이야기 그칠 줄 모르는,

음악 이야기 하다가
또다시 해가 져도

꽃 노래
별 노래
함께 부르는

이런 친구 하나 있었으면

내 마음 둥둥
얼마나 좋을까...

어떤 모순

– 존재증명. 25

머언 산만 바라보다
바윗돌에 부딪혀 터지고

턱밑 땅만 굽어보다
발밑 돌에 채어 넘어지고

직립보행 생멸질서 모르는 이
숲과 나무 함께 볼 순 더욱 없는 것을

짐승으로 추락하는 줄도 모르면서
잔인한 야수가 되어 가는 지구촌

중천의 태양 서녘 산등성 걸리면
문명도 저물어 어두운 그림자 길게 드리울 것을

흑암은 광명을 먹어 삼키고
광명은 흑암을 훼파하느니

정正 반反이 있을 뿐
합습이 없는 혼돈의 땅

새벽 닭울음소리

차마 잊을 수가 없구나.
그날 밤 그 새벽의 그 비탄을

은 삼십에 얻은 천하의 비극

오늘도 그 밤 같은 새벽미명 혼돈과
흑암에 잠긴 적막을 재우쳐 찢으면서

깨어나라, 깨어나라, 깨어나라 ! 새벽마다
울대에 피가 맺히도록 외쳐대는 경성警醒을

차마 새벽잠을 이룰 수가 없구나
왕도 신하도 못 된 나는 어쩌다가

이 땅에 태어나 잃어버린 70년을 살면서
피히테Fichte*의 음성이 새벽마다 들려 우나니

이쩰기나, 어찐거나 저 장내 저내로
다시 70년의 70 곱 세월이 온다면…

* '독일 국민에게 고함' 이란 강연으로 유명한 독일 철학자

가슴이 답답한 까닭
– 존재증명. 4

길이 없는 건 아니다
원주 안에 갇혔거나
사방 감옥에 유폐 되었거나
사방팔방 십 육방 삼십 육방 무한대까지---
길이 없는 건 아니다. 다만
사람의 길과 짐승의 길이 다를 뿐,
육로 해로 항로, 지상의 길과 천상의 길이 있을 뿐,
손가락만 보고 달을 못 보면 달은 없는 것
풍랑으로 요동치는 바다도 이치를 알면 보행
할 수 있고
이치를 모르면 코끼리는 바람벽일 수밖에
눈雪도 물이요 얼음도 물이요 증기와 구름도
물인 것을

숨이 막힌다. 답답하여라.
물을 보고 물이 아니라니
가슴이 터진다. 강물을 틀어막는 이들이여
물은 본시 어떤 장벽 어떤 철벽도 용납지 않음이

그 철칙인 걸 모르는 청맹과니들 가련타.
넘쳐흐르고 스며서 흐르고 구름으로 올랐다 내려 흐르는
그런 물을 기어이 막으려다 기어이 익사하고 마는 가련한 이들이여
물이 곧 길이요 진리요 생명인 걸 아직도 모르시는지---

떠도는 언어 · I

갑자기 하늘 가득
떠도는 언어를 보네
땅 위에서 함부로 쏘아올린
백학처럼 고운 언어들이
학이 되지 못한 채로
주인을 부르네

하늘에서야 눈빛 만으로서도
가슴 속까지 헤아려 보는 곳이어니
아름다운 치장만으로는
어딜 가도 반기는 이 없으리라
그까짓 눈 가린 속셈쯤
모를 리 없으리라

사람 살아가는 일이
어디 그리 쉬우랴만
철만 되면 쏟아지는
수수깡 같은 언어들의 무게를

무엇으로 가늠하랴

미구에 빛바랜 향연이 될
부질없는 서언誓言들로 하여
잠시 헛배가 부르고
꾸역꾸역 헛구역질이 나던 날

강여울 바라보며
〈베네치아의 뱃노래〉를 듣노라면
하나 둘씩 추락하는
까마귀를 보네.

II

새는 작아도 하늘을 난다

새는 작아도 하늘을 난다

시인의 가슴에선
새들이 운다.
봄 여름 가을 겨울에도
새들이 울어댄다.

아니야, 우는 게 아닐 거야
하늘에서 평화를 실어 나르는
코러스, 오라토리오
숲에서 들에서 온통…

천사의 아리아가 끝나면
악마의 소란한 아우성 한바탕
아니야, 그것도 아니야
가만 숨죽이고 들어봐
끝없이 이치는 소리

'미친놈, 미친놈들
날이 밝으면 우리들은 하늘에서

평화를 날라 오지만, 저놈들은 그걸
파괴하기에 바빠'

겸손히 귀 기울여 들어보라고
'부질없어, 부질없어'
자꾸만 애가 잦아 울고 있잖아,

'오늘도 무사하라고
하늘 무너지고 땅 꺼지는 일만은
제발 없도록 하라고'!
산들이 메아리로 울려오고
들판에도 바람결에 울려 퍼진다.

새는 작아도 하늘을 난다.

겨울나무를 보며

– 존재증명. 1

보라 새들의 비가와 조사와
앙상한 가지서 울려오는 레퀴엠을
나무들은 저렇게 겨울을 사는가 보다.

떨며 흔들리며 흩날리다 찢긴
갈 곳도 없는 무수한 유서들을
하릴없이 포도와 들녘에 흩뿌리는
충천하던 거목들의 허무와 무상

인정도 눈물도 증발해버린 염전엔
가슴마다 사막이 된 갈밭 들짐승의
흉흉한 광란뿐 어디에도 착근할 곳 없어
배고픈 기러기처럼 신천옹처럼 하염없이
푸른 달빛 구름 사일 끝없이 허위적이다
어제도 오늘도 내일도 날아가고 있나니

오! 찬란한 태양 작열하는 별이여 빛이여
눈이 부시도록 캄캄한 이 빙하동굴을

비취시라 저 겨울나무들처럼 수축되고
일그러진 존재일지라도 내일엔 다시
소생하는 생명의 근원으로 비춰다오!

작은 행복

별들이 고만고만
안개꽃처럼 피어나는 밤
바람이 하늘하늘
이슬 맺힌 풀잎을 어우른다

까닭 모를 아쉬움에
잠 못 이루는데
새벽이 열리는 창가엔
또 한 생명이 떨어지듯
별똥이 떨어지고
엎드려 울다 잠든 베갯머리
문득 한 음성이 들린다

더 빼앗길 것 없는 사람에게
단 하나
아무도 끝내 뺏을 수 없는 건
바로 새벽이슬 같은 눈물

그것이
나의 행복,
하늘로 통하는
깨끗한 이슬방울

고장 난 컴퓨터

– 존재증명. 2

고장 난 컴퓨터 붙들고 뒤채다가
동짓달 긴긴 밤을 하얗게 새웠다.

치고 두드리고 어르고 토닥여도
끝내 시동侍童 하나 분만치 못하는 밤

영혼 없는 컴퓨터의 냉혹한 쇠붙이 소릴
홰치며 재우치던 계명성이 일갈했다.

천국 없는 오만한 과학자보다야 나는
눈치 없는 천치의 삶이 백번 좋다고!

의무
– 존재증명. 6

의무는 삶의 꽃
꽃 중에 꽃은 들꽃 같은 삶의 꽃
준법은 튼실한 열매 그리고 지복
이 꽃만 피어나면 세상은 온통 꽃동산이다.
새들과 벌 나비 춤추고 노래하며 어우러지는
백합 장미 라일락 천리향 오렌지향기
미풍에 밀려오는 순결,
조화론 평화의 강물 넘치는 지구촌은 모두 낙원
곳곳마다 사람마다 저런 꽃 만발하는 날
그리워라.

꽃 없는 세상은 어두운 폐허
낮도깨비 설치는 컴컴한 토굴막장
무섭고 외롭고 너무 서러운 가슴사막
인정도 눈물도 말라 밭아버린 고비사막
가도 가도 오아시스 종려나무 그늘도 없는 땅

이름도 없이 존재도 없이 스러지는 존재들

폭설에 덮인 큰개불알 풀꽃처럼 애처롭구나.
밤하늘 보랏빛별들 쏟아지며 반짝이는
오! 거룩한 손 묵언수도의 꽃향기여

한발旱魃
– 존재증명. 3

하늘에 사무친다. 목이 타는 아우성
자식농사 그르쳐 다 죽게 됐다고.

산 들 강에 파닥거리며 숨 쉬던 것들
소리 없는 몸부림에 천지가 요동친다.
치산치수 관리들 모두 어디 갔느냐고
강 건너 불구경 나리들 아직 국정수행 중
들려오는 메아리…
(웃기지 말라 우리가 누군데…)
개점휴업 무노동 무임금은 어디에 탄하랴?

오! 무심한 하늘이여 땅이여 이제 그만
이 땅의 살인가뭄 진노 푸시고, 금수강산
근역삼천리 어진 백성들 지구촌 구석구석
물은 곧 생명인 것을 진정 깨닫게 하소서
우라늄 플루토늄 잡을 소화기를 주소서!

비인간非人間
– 존재증명. 8

나는 아직 사람이 아니다
오로지 사람이 되고 싶어 한恨 이지만
쉽게 풀길이 없어 밤마다 뒤채다 샌다.
대형서점엔 문턱이 닳도록 드나들며
거친 목재들을 구해 깎고 갈고 다듬고 밀어서
세워봤지만, 살만한 존재의 집 한 채 아직 없으니
나는 사람이 아닌 거다. 그런 내가 또 무엇인지
내 역사를 해명도 못하는 의무불이행의
궁지에서 허위적이고 만 있으니 어찌 사람이랴
위대한 시인은 더욱 언감생심이다.
이목구비 모양 모두 갖추었지만
불행한 사람들 가슴 등 다독이고
빼저린 눈물 닦아주며 행복 한 아름
안겨주지 못하면서
우주의 생명질서도 살아가는 이유도
확증하지 못하면서
어느 시절에 사람 같은 시인이 될 것인가?!
어느 시절에 시인 같은 사람이 될 것인가?!
사람이여 개짐승 같은 사람들이여

청맹과니들

찢기고
꺾이고
할퀴고
뿌리째 뽑힌 모습
어찌 비바람만의 탓이랴

우리들 마음 갈기갈기
찢기고
꺾이고
할퀴어
뿌리째 흔들리는 지구촌

황망히 드리우는 문명의
검은 그림자에 새겨지는
지엄한 잠언을 새겨들을 줄 모르는
눈도 귀도 다 멀어버린 물신의 노예들

피도 눈물도 말라버린 갈밭의

비열한 짐승들 종착은 어딘지
두렵고 무서운 저 속빈 갈대들 군집群集한
도도한 물결 파도쳐 밀려오는 위력
숨통이 꽉 막혀 터지는 별들의 전쟁....

태초의 동산을 잃어버린 게 언제던가?
사람의 가슴, 마음, 영혼, 정신, 창조주의
자리에 모조리 사물인터넷을 장착해
황량한 거대 사막을 확장하는 무리들!

지하철 승강장에서

저것은 전동차가 아니다.
기항지를 알리는 원양어선의 고동소리
나는 아직도 풋내기 어부.

온갖 생각 구름처럼 피었다 지는 선상
밟히고 부딪히고 찢기면서 가는
먼 바다 무서운 롤링과 피칭에 떨지만
오직 만선과 무사 귀항을 빌 뿐,

조약돌이 되고 모래가 되더라도
경각의 시간, 녹아내리는 애간장이야
눈부신 진주 루비 하나 양생하리니…

한강 야경

불빛이 흐른다
강물 위에

문명이 흐르는 피안엔
허무가 쌓이는데

별빛 어른어른 쏟아져도
실향민의 추억은 서럽고

멀리 수은등 푸른 불빛이
국경인 양 가슴 시리다

무언가
넘치는 술잔 부딪히는 소리는

지축이 흔들리는 듯
바벨탑 무너지는 소리

새벽이 열리는 창가

밤새 은하를 항진한 조각배 한 척
세사에 저린 눈빛으로
서녘 산등성에
닻을 내리면
누군가 가없는 사랑으로
대지를 포옹하고
어둠을 털며 기침起寢하는
발자국소리 들린다.

흑암을 반추하면
은백색 부활은 잉태하는 것이어늘
무언가 다시
암울한 혼돈으로 반전하는 것은

새벽이 열리는 창가에
귀를 기울이면
마지막 그날 밤 닭울음소리
베드로의 한숨소리 들리는 듯, 여기

사겁四劫을 맴도는 땅 한 구석
웬일로 이 새벽
소쩍새는 저리 목이 메이고
유성은 산 너머로 지는가.

남향한 창문 하나

남향한 창문 하나 있어
나는 살아가네.

밤새껏
어둠속 헤매다가
피곤한 영혼으로
새벽을 맞으면
언제나 스며드는 한 줄기 빛이 있어
오늘도 내 영혼 살아나네.

남향한 내 작은 창가
마음을 기대면
하늘은 언제나 파랗게 열리고
구름은 부풀어
숨통이 트이네
하늘끝 이르네

남향한 내 작은 창문 하나 없었던들
내 어찌 살아갈 수 있으랴....

고향풍경

흙 담장 돌아서면
쇠죽냄새 외양간

탱자 울 사립문 사이
흘러나는 사랑방 불빛

오늘도 손짓하며 부르는
나직한 목소리들

떠돌다 지친 나그네
귓전을 때리네.

제비꽃

마음 황망한 사람에겐
눈길 주지 않는
수줍은 연심
부시도록
신비한 전설들을 안고
호젓한 곳 찾아내려
별무리 반짝이듯
소곤대는 귀엣말

한사코
세상 너무
요란하다고,
질경이 돌나물 씀바귀....
옛 벗이 그립다고
쏟아놓는 노래여
분향粉香 같은 순결이여

치솟는 빌딩가에 어쩌다 남아

벽돌 새 비집고
잃어버린 전원을 노래 부르며
실바람에 하늘하늘
아스팔트 지열地熱에 눈먼
도심都心을 깨우는가.

눈 속에 피는 풀꽃
– 존재증명. 18

폭설이 녹은 틈새로 어느새 솟아오른
보랏빛 들풀꽃잎 하나 보는 순간
그만 감전되듯 소스라쳤네.

만성 간염과 위염 신경성 질병을 앓다가
찾은 심산계곡 호숫가 언덕에서 만난 풀꽃
그건 무명 잡초 아닌 신이 내린 약초였으리.

그 풀꽃 들고 여기저기 알아보다가
식물도감에서 본 이름은 "큰개불알풀"
그 풀꽃 줄기 꺾어 병실 머리맡에 두고

종일토록 주문을 외듯
대화하며 사랑에 빠져들었네.
신통한 생명력이 유입되도록.

마침내 편작扁鵲이도 못 당할
죽음의 사신을 물리친 나는 지금도
겨울이면 그를 찾아 눈길을 걷곤 하네.

III

문명의 그늘

문명의 그늘

1. 투명한 새끼달팽이의 죽음에 대한 조사弔辭

아- 슬프도다. 오늘이여
어쩌다 미물로 태어나
인간 세상 들렀다가
초록빛 나무그늘 강물처럼 흐르는 고향
그리던 부모형제 멀리 두고 가다니 !
우주의 생명질서는
지구촌 생명질서는
생명 있는 것은 무엇이나
생존할 가치가 있는 것을
더불어, 함께 살 권리가 있는 것을
만물의 영장이란 오만한 인류의
독선과 지배 앞에서,
문명을 모르는 지구촌 가족들은
생존권을 박탈당하는
약육강식의 세상에서
너의 생존환경을 마련 못한 우리의 죄
용서하고 잘 가거라
고이 잠 사서라 투명한 새끼 달팽이야 !

* 마무그늘 : '나무그늘'로 고쳐 번역함

문명의 그늘

2. 투명한 새끼달팽이의 비문碑文

여기 목련화 그늘
장미화 수선화 모란과 칸나가
번갈아 피고 지는 화단 양지쪽
실향한 투명한 새끼달팽이
영원히 고이 잠들다

태초에 조물주의 뜻 있어
투명한 새끼달팽이
인간 세상 함께 살았네

너도 나도 가면으로 포장한
문명세계 어두운 곳 돌아다니며
몸도 마음도 하나 같이 투명한
광명정대한 삶의
정도正道를 보여주다가

비가 오면 비에 젖고
바라 불면 바람 맞고

곳간도 없이 창고도 없이
투명한 옷 한 벌 그대로
살아생전 죄업 없이 살다가

밤에는 별빛 어린 호숫가에
낮에는 햇살 부신 초원에서
흙냄새 풀냄새 들이쉬며
풀잎의 감로수를 마시며
여한 없이 행복하게 살다가

몰아닥친 개발붐에
마구 뿌린 살충제에
중독되어 피 마르고
신경세포 파괴되어
항변 한번 못 한 채로
쓸쓸하게 죽어가다

이에
문명의 독소를 경계하여
지구촌의 종말을 막으려 함이니
오는 이 가는 이 모두 보고
삼가 투명한 새끼달팽이의 교훈을
새길지니….

파도가 들려준 귀엣말

숨 막히도록 짓누르던
일상의 늪에서 탈출하다
남해의 작은 섬에
잠시 내 인생선의
작은 닻을 내리고
하늘 이 끝에서 하늘 저 끝까지
쉼 없이 밀려왔다 밀려가는
파도소리 듣다가
문득 뒤돌아본다. 아스라이 지나온 항로
산산히 부서졌다가 자맥질하며 다시 일어나던

삶은 정녕 파도 같은 것
수유도 한 자리 머무를 수 없이
모든 것은 떠도는 것을
섬에 와서 보니 섬도 섬으로 아니 뵈고
뭍 또한 섬에 다름 아닌 것
내 지금껏 보고 들은 것 모두
착시현상이요 착각일레라

세상 어디에도 흔들리지 않는 것 없음에
세상 무엇이나 흘러가지 않는 것도 없네
강물도 흘러가고
바다도 흘러가고
바람도 구름도
사랑도 꿈도 흐르고 흘러감이여
나 얼마나 여기 더 머무를 수 있을까
이 작은 섬에서

야자수 그늘 시원하고
파초의 옷소매 요염하게 유혹하는데
내 작은 배 닻줄 언제까지
고정되어 있을까
바람은
파도는
어느만큼 자애로울까.

백사장에서

보아라
절벽과 낭떠러지의 바위들과
깊은 바다 밑 암초들까지
분말 같은 모래가 되는 여정旅程을

태풍에 밀리고
파도에 찢기고
본시 현상 가뭇없이
티끌로 사라지면서
자유자재 운신運身의 모습을

보아라
제 목소리도 없고
제 색깔조차 다 바래버린
그러다가 은빛 백사장에
그림자를 드리우는 구름처럼
어느 순간 소멸해버리는 것을

그리고 다시 또 보아라
모래처럼 많은 발자국들
파도에 밀려 쌓이는 피미披靡를!

한강 유람선 상에서

– 24회 세계시인대회 3일째 밤

흐르는 것은 강물이 아니다
흐르는 것은 평화요 사랑이요 시의 물결이다
온 세계 온 인류가 만나기 위한
더 큰 바다로 흐르는 시의 물결이다

창밖의 휘황한 저것은 가로등이 아니다
어둠을 몰아내는 저것은
진리요 지혜요 더불어 살아가라는
하늘의 빛살이다
가슴마다, 가슴마다 품고 피워내야 할
타오르는 횃불이다

전쟁을, 시기를, 질투를 추방하려는
우리들 가슴 가슴의 아름다운 꽃불이다

흐르는 것은
한강의 물결만이 아니다
휘황한 것은
서울 야경의 불빛만이 아니다

떠도는 언어. III
– 존재증명. 10

사랑하는 나의 시편들이여 영혼이여
지금쯤 어느 하늘밑 떠돌며 울고 있느냐

허허벌판 쑥대밭 산비탈이거나 북천
기러기 떼 끼룩끼룩 나는 겨울밤을

시베리아 설원 '겨울 나그네' 처럼 나그네처럼
외투깃에 고개를 묻고 어깨엔 기타를 메고

개들이 컹컹대는 어두운 발길을 홀로 쓸쓸히
하늘 향해 영혼의 노래를 부르며 가고 있느냐

사랑도 열정도 연인도 벗도 따르는 자도 없이
음악에 미쳐 음악에 미쳐 지칠 대로 지쳐 혼곤한

예술의 혼과 더불어 저녁불빛도 다정스런 십
우편마차를 달려 까마귀 우는 숲을 지나

이정표도 없어 초조한 마음으로 휴식할 곳을
찾고 있느냐 곱은 손 호호 불며 방황하느냐

오! 이제 그만 편히 쉬어라 얼어붙은 눈물 씻고
봄꿈을 찾아 봄꿈을 찾아 편히 쉬어라 나의 시
편들아

철지난 장미를 보며

10월도 하순
또 한 해의 저물녘
마른 잎은 흩날려 어디로 가는지

후미진 산기슭 노을 슬픈 곳 지키며
파르르 부르르 떨며 흔들리는 모습 서러워
기러기도 푸른 달빛 시린 하늘을
기럭기럭 울면서 날아갔나 보다

유폐된 폐비처럼 화려한 왕관도 내려놓고
몰락한 왕자처럼 찬란한 영화도 벗어놓고
떠나는 모습 덧없고 가여워서
귀뚜리도 풀숲 찬 서리 맞으며
눈물의 시를 밤새 읊었나보다.

태양의 언덕에 다시 훈풍이 불면
겹겹의 화려한 꽃잎 피어날까
황홀한 향기 다시 날려 올까

황홀한 비가

1. 외로운 국운선國運船

아 - 찬란한 역사의 빛
이제 그만 스러지는가
캄캄한 환란의 구름
언제까지 덮치려는가
반만 년 긴긴 역사
동방의 등불인데
추락한 신인도信認度는
천년 두고 한이어라
산 같이 드높은 기상
헛된 꿈이 되려는가

아 - 험난한 이 항로여
밀려오는 만경창파여
외로운 국운선은
위태로이 요동치네
깨어나라 민족혼아
이 시대 등불이여
온 세계 주시하는

냉혹한 눈길 보아라
찬연한 우리의 역사
다시 한 번 빛내보자.

어떤 진화

– 존재증명. 7

머리에서 스파크가 번쩍번쩍 튄다.
페스트 에이즈 에볼라 콜레라 메르스---
예측불허의 가공할 적들의 침략전쟁

노벨의 유언을 까맣게 잊은 존재망각의
끝없는 반복을 유형화하는 물신노예들,
저렇듯 불량의 번식을 속수무책으로
오늘도 내일도 그 다음날도 방조하리니

정신 차릴진저 '불량의 번식을 돕는 것은
사실상 후손들에게 수많은 적들을 물려주는
고약한 짓, 적자가 생존하기 위해서는 악자의
번식을 막아야 한다.'는 경구를 명심하도록!

리트머스 시험지
– 존재증명. 11

슬플 땐 눈물 피잉 돌다가
기쁠 땐 웃음 펑펑 터지는
싫으면 버럭 화를 내놓고
좋으면 금방 어린 아이로
진정제라도 먹어야겠다.

청색은 하늘 적색은 태양
명광과 혼탁 진리와 역리
우주 만물의 생명 질서를
어찌 두 색만으로 분별할까
정녕 진정제를 먹어야겠다.

다시 하늘로. 4

다시 하늘로 깃을 치며 날아오르라
유유창천 종달새처럼 앨버트로스처럼 !

폭염과 태풍과 폭우와 해일에 쫓기던 너희들
꼬이고 뒤틀리고 찢기고 구겨진 혼돈의 숲에
갈 곳을 잃은, 쉴 곳도 잃은 백의의 천사들아 !

날마다 각다귀판 소동으로 하늘 길 통로가
꽉막혀버린 통한의 철벽 70년을 어이하랴
"불량종의 번식을 돕는 것은 후손들에게
수많은 적들을 물려주는 고약한 짓"인 것을…

황금과 권세, 거짓 술수에 눈도 귀도 멀어버린
갈밭 야수들아
슬픔 같은 것, 눈물 같은 것, 원망, 핑계로,
회칠한 호화별장
어디에도 너희들 숨을 곳은 없나니
이제 그만 스러져다오

침몰한 국운선國運船 창문을 두드리며
쥐어뜯는 비명 절규
밤바다 새벽마다 환청으로 들으면서,
들으면서 기구하나니

시방, 동토 헤치고 부활한 가녀린 보리 낟들
새로운 생명으로 웃자라 춤추는 춘삼월인데
종달새는 목련꽃 져버린 하늘을 구가하는데
복마전 넓은 초원에서 황금 술잔이나 들면서
3, 4, 5, 6월 같은 잔인한 세월만 살 것인가?

서두르지 않아도 되는 것을

잠시 하늘 보며 심호흡,
한 걸음 뒤져 기다릴 순 없을까

사소한 양보가 뜻밖의
큰 재앙을 밀쳐내느니

조급한 마음이여 옆치기는 말자구나
그리고 기억하자구나 평생토록 !

천년 같은 하루 서둘다가
찰나에 날아갈 줄 누가 알리오.

참된 평화와 행복을
초침으로 계산할 순 없나니

시인에게

시인이여
당신의 눈은 번갯불이외다.
눈 깜짝할 사이
온 우주 훑어보는
무서운 번갯불

당신의 머리는 칼이외다.
그 예날 솔로몬이 심판을 하듯
한칼에 목을 칠 수도 있는
차갑게 섬광 짓는 칼

당신의 마음은 태양이외다.
팔천 도 구천 도 사랑으로 이글거리는
불덩이,
무쇠 돌멩이 더러운 얼음덩이도
단숨에 녹여버리는 용광로

당신의 가슴은 옹달샘이외다.

어머님 젖가슴 같이
언제나 부드러운 생명수 솟고
오가는 나그네
거기 쉬다
돌아가는 길목에 항상
넘치는 생명의 샘물

당신의 숨결은 천사의 합창이외다.
거룩하고 순결한 환희에 넘쳐
쏟아놓는 칸타타 토카타
지옥 잠을 깨우는 새벽 종소리

당신은 고달픈 임산부외다.
먹고 입고 거하는데 삼가 삼백 날
한 생명 속으로 키우며
입덧으로 마냥 괴로워하는
임산부

당신은 이제 등대외다.
칠흑 같은 밤
북두칠성 별빛도 없는 망망대해의
허우적거리는 무리 속
거기 우뚝 서서

밤새도록 쉬지 않고 비추는 등대

당신은 마침내 나팔수외다.
산을 울리고 들을 울려
저 수평선 너머 하늘끝 메아리로
돌아올 때까지
한껏 불어대야 할 나팔수
시인이여!

처서 處暑

콩밭에 이는 바람
어느새 지열을 식히고

산그늘 수수밭
새들도 바쁘게 날아간다.

바람처럼 무심한 것과
구름처럼 변전하는 것들을

무어라 그리도
혼신으로 사랑하다가

못 견디게 그리운 것과
사무치게 한스러운 것들을 그대로 두고

여름이 가듯 그렇게
차마 그렇게 떠날 수는 없거늘

작열하던 가슴 강물로 흐르려 해도
끝없이 밀려와 파도치는 그리움

차라리 바위 되어 한생전 잊으려 해도
속 깊이 파고들어 뒤흔드는 외로움

숲속엔 매미들 절박하게 우는 소리
귓전엔 어디서 들려오는 세레나데.

그리움

오오 내 사랑 어디 갔나
한 마디 말도 없이
멀리서 돌아보면
못 견디게 기룰 것을
해질녘 그리움이야
파도처럼 높으이다.

높깊은 정을 두고
떠나가면 어이하리
기어이 가실거면
마음마저 거둘 것을
차라리 이 마음이야
죽음도곤 아프이다

그리운 사람이여
어느 하늘 계시는가
빈 하늘 뜬 구름만
바람결에 쓸쓸한데
이 저녁 외로움이야
생각사록 애달프오

Ⅳ

그날은 언젠가?

그날은 언젠가?

고도 3454미터 융프라우요흐,
처녀와 봉우리의 만남이란 이름의
만년설 정상, 빙하의 트래킹과
설상 산책, 스핑크스의 테리스
얼음궁진 돌아보다 소스라쳐
백두산천지 생각에 제 정신 들었네.

만족의 영산 천지호수 노천온천까지
하룻길에 오고 갈 수 있는 금수강산을
철책으로 가로막은지 고희가 넘도록
두더지처럼 밤낮 땅굴이나 파고
지뢰나 묻으면서
동족의 머리위에 폭탄이나 쏟으려
광분하는 자들아
대답을 하라! 제 정신 차릴 날이 언젠가?

우라늄 플루토늄은 불타는 지옥문 입구일 뿐
공멸의 망상이요 영화의 허상인 걸 모르는가?

멸망의 어두운 유령 탈을 벗어버리고
잃었던 나라 되찾던 그날처럼 황소타고
풍악 울리며 황금들판 누비던 그날처럼
참 광복의 노래를, 통일만세를 불러보자 !

그날이 오면, 정녕 근역삼천리 한길로 열리면
백두에서 한라까지 평화의 봇물 터지기만 하면
융프라우요가 부러우랴 영세중립국이 부러우랴
대답을 하라! 과학자 정치가 백만장자들아 우린
언제 어느 날 백의민족의 얼을 회복할 수 있는지?

타임아웃

언제쯤, 누가 어느 시절에
휘슬 울리는 날이 올 수는 있을까?
금성金聲이 스치는 순간 스러지는
자연하던 태양처럼 폭염처럼
별들의 전쟁까지 일시 선에
합리성과 자유의지 남용하는
갈발 들짐승들, 비열한 강자독식 게임
타임아웃 휘슬 불어줄 심판은 없을까

흑백의 전도 선악의 전도顚倒,
전도의 악순환 확대재생산 끝없이
평화를 전쟁으로 조화를 갈등으로
행복을 불행으로 번영을 폐망으로
자유를 방종으로 다양성을 혼란으로 달리는
양두구육 술수와 비열한 사람이여 지성들이여
인류역사상 무식하고 가난한자는 큰 전쟁을
일으킨 저 없나니, 정녕 없나니…

과학은 별들의 큰 전쟁을 불러오고
정치는 이기야욕을 위한 야단법석*일 뿐,
수단방법불문하고 치부에 미친 졸부들까지
득실득실 옥외화장실 구더기처럼
속빈 갈대숲처럼 군집群集한 위력으로
사특한 술수의 궤변으로 세상을 망쳐
더 이상 설 자리 없어 떠도는 이방인은
갈 곳을 잃었노라! 잃어버린 우리 낙원
어느 시절 어디 가서 찾을 수 있는가?!
목성인木星人들은 지구촌 인간들 악취에
지구엔 접근조차 못하고 떠돈다던데(?)...

심판이여, 공정한 심판이여 제발, 추악한 속임수
지구촌 게임 이제 그만 휘슬을 불어다오!
지구촌 다 썩고 다른 별까지 오염되기 전,
문명의 음산한 그늘 무섭게 덮치기 전에!

* 야단은 야기요단(惹起鬧端)의 준말. 서로 시비의 실마리를 끌어 내어 소동을 일으킴을 뜻함.

또 다른 출발. 2

다시 또 어디엔들
새로운 출발선이 있을까?
해가 바뀌고 계절이 바뀌었는데
갈 곳이 없다. 돌아보면 아스라한
고빗사위길 반환점밖에 없으니, 애달픈들
어이하랴. 흉흉한 소문만 무성해 믿을 곳도
의지할 곳도 없는 노인충蟲들
잠자리 들기 전엔 기구, 자고새면 매양
두 주먹 불끈 쥐고 새아침 달려보지만 이젠
허공을 달리는 깃털처럼 무중력의 몸짓
겨울비속 노가리는 절대고독의 언덕길을
파릇파릇 하늘거리는 보리피리와 추수 끝낸
모포기마다 파란 싹들이 돋아 어루만진다.

출발선이 기다리던 게 축복인 걸 알듯 하다.
헐떡이며, 헐떡이며 지하철로 버스로 건널목
육교 승상장을 오르내리며 찬물처럼 밀려오고
간물처럼 빠져나가던 날들의 출발선
거기 내 설 자린 이제 정녕 없는가?

내가 그리는 집

남으로 창을 낸
작은 집을 지으리라

문 열면 언제라도
산과 바다가
들어오는 곳

밤이면 별들이 내려와
머나먼 고향얘기 풀어놓고
낮이면 산바람 지나가며
막힌 가슴 트여주는 곳

가을 봄 여름 없이
들꽃들이 저마다
투명한 햇살을 안고
하늘대며 조아리는 곳

내
영원한 집을 지으리라

물소리 바람소리
새소리 벌레소리
어우러 살아가는
울 없는 집을.

가을

바람
휩쓸고 간 자리
세월 그림자
설다

늦가을
비 내린다
갈 숲에서 푸드득
들새 한 마리
길 잃은
철새

머언 산
땅거미
밀려온다.

살며 후회하며

살며 후회하며 시를 쓴다.
때론 황량한 들판에 홀로 서서
소나기 한 바탕 없는
뜨거운 열기에 지치고
때론 빙판길을 애쓰며 걸어왔다

지는 해 돋는 달
언제 한 번 바라볼 겨를 있었던가
쫓기듯 도망치듯 앞만 보고 살아왔다

돌아보면 아득하여라
걸어온 길마다
서린 아픔 서린 눈물 이슬로 맺혀
바람이 불어오면
덧없이 땅으로 돌아가는 것을

한 고개를 넘으면
그 땐 그 모든 것
기쁨도 슬픔도 되는 것을.

길손

우리는 길손
자고나면 다시
어디론지 떠나야 할 명운命運,

건널목을 지나
산으로 들로
신호등 따라오는 순명順命,

넘어야 할 산
건너야 할 물
오늘도 내일도 그렇게

어딜 가면
어둔 길 함께 갈
길동무 만날 수 있을까

창窓

외로움 반추하면
별빛 찾아들고

사무쳐 모로 누면
달빛 새어 드는 곳

꿈을 앗긴 쓰라림
기를 꺾인 생채기

바람은 스쳐가며 매만지고
구름은 지나가며 위로하는 곳

들피진 여로에서 돌아와
곤비한 영혼 하늘 보며 쉬는 곳

날마다 치솟는 담장들
길길이 가로막아 서더라도

늘인 목 먼 산 바라보며
고향하늘 달려가는 곳

고향

머언 마을
개 짖는 소리
창호지 문살을 울리면
가물가물
흔들리는 호롱불
반백의 머리칼에
잃어버린 고향집이 되살아난다.

함박눈이 펑펑
쏟아지는 저녁
장독대엔
시집간 누나
발자국이 살아나고,

어디선가 불쑥
다가서는 고향 그림자
달빛 밝아 잠 못 이루는데

못 잊어
못 잊어
눈 모으면 다시
가슴 시린 달빛.

숲을 보며. 5

다시 어둠이 내리는 숲을 본다
소소한 바람결에 들리는 비창을
듣는다

차마 볼 수 없는 폐허,
바다 건거 무역센터와 펜타곤의 빌딩숲까지
21세기 바벨탑의 형해가 되어버리던 날
포세이돈과 허리케인의 검붉은 용들의
광란 앞에서 나는

피에타 시뇨레(pieta Signore*)!
이 한 곡 진혼의 노래라도 바쳐 올리면
태풍에 할퀸 생채기 아물 수 있을까
숲의 나라 백성들 산발한 채 흐느끼는
몸부림과 터져 흐르는 혈흔에
바위조차 떨고 있는 빈소마다,

백두대간 산허리도 갈기갈기
찢어발기는 바람은 지긋지긋
이제 그만
진저리가 난다. 광란의 그 바람
때만 되면 그칠 줄 모르는 미친바람!
또 다시 일어나면 흉흉한 소문 소문들
먹구름처럼 떼 지어 밀려오고 덮쳐
숲엔 다시 어둠이 내리는데
별빛마저 가려져 신비한
전설마저 들을 수 없는 세상

* A. Stradella의 성가곡聖歌曲

춘경春耕

– 존재증명. 23

갈수록 거친 들녘
소 몰아 논밭 갈던 시절
하 그립구나.

봄갈이 때를 잃으면
도둑처럼 봄날은 가고
강도처럼 설한풍 밀어닥치는 것을
그날의 허기와 한기에 찬 곳간
누가 무엇으로 채울 수 있으랴

가도 가도 기계소리 풍성한 묵정밭
이 봄에도 엉겅퀴와 가시덤불
무성히 하늘을 덮고 있을까
심는 대로 거두는 것을

지금, 갈아엎고 골라내고
피와 땀과 눈물의 참된
씨앗 뿌리지 않으면
텅 빈 곳간 채울 것은
세상 어디에도 OO 없는 것을.

파종播種의 노래

나는 씨 뿌리는 농부
이방 산천 유벽한 곳

가시덤불 자갈밭을
뽑아내고 골라내고
좋은 씨만 파종하는
외롭지만 참 행복한,

봄바람이 산들 불면
들꽃들은 하늘하늘
산새들이 노래하면
시냇물도 도란도란

아름다운 이 세상을
모두 함께 만들고자
삼십 비, 육 십 배,
백배 소출 기원하는

커피 한 잔

커피 한 잔
마주 놓으면
마음은 마음으로 이어지고
사랑은 사랑으로 이어지는 것

커피 한 잔
진하디 진한 커피 한 잔
못하는 마음이야
너무나 안타까운 가난한 마음

커피 한 잔 못 나누고
쫓기듯 돌아오는 날은
사는 맛이 소태 같구나

사람은 쓴 잔을
함께 나누며
살아가야 하는 것을.

꿈꾸는 소리

아리울*에서

들려온다. 꿈꾸는 소리
바다가 육지로 태어나는
아스란 지평선 저 너머서
밤새도록 찰싹이던 소리
새 생명 잉태하는 저 소리
하나 둘 금빛 파도에 실려
밀려오는 저 소리 아- 아-
평화와 번영 밀려오는 저 소리

들려온다. 꿈꾸는 소리
조용한 아침의 나라 여기
아스란 수평선 저 너머서
종일토록 속삭이는 소리
새 생명 태어나는 저 소리
하나 둘 은빛 물결에 실려
고동치는 저 소리 이- 이-
동방의 등불 타오르는 저 소리

들려온다. 꿈꾸는 소리
세계만민 더불어 살아갈
드넓고 드맑은 저 너머서
새로운 문명 움트는 소리
온갖 시름 물러가는 소리
오로지 인류애의 꽃으로
피어나는 저 소리 아- 아-
하늘이여 땅이여 바닷길이여

* 새만금 간척사업현장을 지칭함.

추억

주린 배 채운 하늘
타는 목 축인 별빛

가난도 지난 후면
추어 한 줌 되는 것을

솔바람 말도 없이
장공을 지나가는데

태풍에 찢긴 날개
호숫가에 잠들리.

60 Selected Poems of

Seo Jeong-Nam

A Gold Beetle's Nostalgia

서정남 시선집(제9집)

풍뎅이의 향수 鄕愁

인쇄일 | 2016년 9월 30일
발행일 | 2016년 9월 30일

지은이 | 서정남
펴낸곳 | 도서출판 조은
발행인 | 김화인
편집인 | 김진순
주소 | 서울 중구 을지로20길 12, 405호(인현동1가, 대성빌딩)
전화 | (02)2273-2408
팩스 | (02)2272-1391
출판등록 | 1995년 7월 5일 등록번호 제2-1999호
ISBN | 978-89-94329-92-5
정가 | 15,000원